Chinua
Achebe

by ARTHUR RAVENSCROFT

Published for the British Council
and the National Book League
by Longmans, Green & Co

Three shillings and sixpence net

'Three or four weeks ago my wife, who teaches English in a boys' school, asked a pupil why he wrote about winter when he meant the harmattan. He said he would be laughed out of class if he did such a thing! Now, you wouldn't have thought, would you, that there was something shameful in your weather? But apparently we do. How can this great blasphemy be purged? I think it is part of my business as a writer to teach that boy that there is nothing disgraceful about the African weather, that the palm-tree is a fit subject for poetry . . .' This was Chinua Achebe speaking at a conference on Commonwealth Literature held in Leeds in 1964. In all his novels, most notably in his first, *Things Fall Apart*, Achebe has been concerned with what he described as 'the traumatic effects of our first confrontation with Europe'. The clash of the two cultures is revealed not only in the themes he chooses—the impact of white missionaries on a tribal society, as in *Things Fall Apart*, the return of a European-educated Nigerian to a job in Lagos in *No Longer at Ease*—but in the use of a wide range of language from Ibo to Pidgin and English enriched with vivid Ibo proverbs.

Chinua Achebe was born at Ogidi near Onitsha in Eastern Nigeria in 1930. His mother-tongue was Ibo though he learned some English for his father was the teacher in charge of the Church Missionary Society's village school. In 1953 he was one of the first students to graduate from the University College in Ibadan. In 1954 he became Talks Producer for the Nigerian Broadcasting Series and in 1961 he was appointed Director of External Broadcasting for Nigeria. In 1966, after the massacre of Ibos in Northern Nigeria, he moved to the Eastern Region where he was preparing to go into a new publishing venture when war broke out.

The best of Achebe's writing is not restricted to commentary on his own society but is an instrument 'for analyzing tragic experience and profound human issues of very much more than local Nigerian significance', as Mr Ravenscroft writes of *Things Fall Apart*, probably the most outstanding work yet produced by this gifted writer.

Mr Ravenscroft is a graduate of the universities of Cape Town and Cambridge, and has lectured in English in the universities of Cape Town and Stellenbosch, the University College of Salisbury, Rhodesia and, since 1963, the University of Leeds where he is senior lecturer in English literature. He translated the third volume of *Van Riebeeck's Journal* (1952) with C. K. Johnman and has been editor of *The Journal of Commonwealth Literature* since it was founded in 1965.

CHINUA ACHEBE
by
Arthur Ravenscroft

Edited by Ian Scott-Kilvert

Dotun Okunbanjo

CHINUA ACHEBE

CHINUA
ACHEBE

by

ARTHUR RAVENSCROFT

PUBLISHED FOR
THE BRITISH COUNCIL
AND THE NATIONAL BOOK LEAGUE
BY LONGMANS, GREEN & CO

LONGMANS, GREEN & CO LTD
Longman House, Burnt Mill, Harlow, Essex
*Associated companies, branches and
representatives throughout the world*

First published 1969
© Arthur Ravenscroft 1969

*Printed in Great Britain by
F. Mildner & Sons, London, EC1*

Acknowledgment: Thanks are due to Chinua Achebe's publishers, William
Heinemann Ltd, for permission to quote from works in copyright.

CHINUA ACHEBE

I

FOR centuries London has been a metropolis for writers born in the British Isles, and by the second half of the nineteenth century it was also attracting aspirant writers from the imperial provinces abroad, like Olive Schreiner from the Cape Colony, who first went to London in 1881 and had her novel, *The Story of an African Farm*, published there in 1883. To London also came writers from the United States, notably Henry James, and, in the twentieth century, Robert Frost and T. S. Eliot.

That one of the greatest English novelists since the 1890s was a Pole by birth and far more French than English by education is an historical irony which cannot be ascribed to the attraction exerted by the metropolis upon an imperially distended area of influence. Joseph Conrad's years in the British mercantile marine and his anglophile sentiments must have had a great deal to do with his writing in English rather than French.

Since the 1930s there has come into existence a body of writing in English by authors who cannot be thought of simply as writers from the overseas provinces, though in fact, like their contemporaries, Roy Campbell from South Africa and Katherine Mansfield from New Zealand, they were natives of distant parts of the British Empire, as it then was. What differentiates them as a group from Australians, Canadians, New Zealanders and some South Africans, is that, like Conrad, they chose to write in English rather than in their mother tongues. Before the Second World War the best known of them were Indians—Mulk Raj Anand's first novel, *Untouchable*, appeared in 1935, as did R. K. Narayan's *Swami and Friends*; Raja Rao's *Kanthapura* was published in 1938. Again, unlike Conrad, they did not look with the sort of approval evinced by Marlow in the 1890s at those areas of the global map usually shaded red. In India they were in one way or another associated with the

Nationalist Movement for freedom, though Narayan explains his use of the imperial language by pointing out simply, and without bitterness, that it was the language he became most familiar with from his earliest school-days. What more natural than to use it when he began to write? Although Mulk Raj Anand spent many years in England and Raja Rao in Paris (and more recently the United States), they and Narayan can hardly be thought of as British writers. They have not severed their Indian roots, and this shows clearly in the novels they have written. In trying to convey Indian experience in English and in Indian-English words, they have been forced to develop the English novel in ways sometimes refreshingly and vitally different from those of the British metropolis.

Since the Second World War, at least two other groups of writers in English have been published, whose backgrounds and relationships with Britain are more akin to those of Indians than to those of writers like Patrick White of Australia or Margaret Laurence of Canada. They are the English writers of the Caribbean and of anglophone Africa. This is not the place to consider how much the West Indian novelists in fact have in common with the Indian, Pakistani, and African writers, for the British Caribbean territories do not have long-established literatures in other indigenous languages. In India, Pakistan and Africa writing in English takes place alongside literary activity in languages like Tamil, Bengali, Urdu, Yoruba, etc., and of course it would be very wrong to assume that all educated writers in these countries write in English.

II

The first post-war West African writer to attract attention outside Africa was Amos Tutuola, whose book, *The Palm-Wine Drinkard*, was published in London in 1952. Tutuola writes a highly idiosyncratic English modified by linguistic characteristics of Yoruba (his mother tongue) and Pidgin. The enthusiasm with which his books were first greeted owed more to their 'quaintness' and exoticism than to any real experimental use of language or sense of overall structure and integrated meaning; among students of African literature there is still controversy about whether Tutuola can be considered a serious literary artist. Since the 1950s there has been an ever-increasing stream of books in English by Africans (especially Nigerians) who have been educated in the post-war universities of Africa or in British universities. Novels by Cyprian Ekwensi (born 1921), Chinua Achebe (born 1930) and James Ngugi (born 1938), plays by Wole Soyinka (born 1935) and John Pepper Clark (born 1935), and poems by Soyinka and Christopher Okigbo (1932–67) have appeared in the reading lists of schools examination boards in Africa, and of English departments in African, British, and American universities. Of the African novelists who write in English, Chinua Achebe is perhaps the most considerable.

Achebe was born at Ogidi not far from Onitsha in Eastern Nigeria on 15 November 1930. His mother-tongue was Ibo but he would have learned some English at home as his father, Isaiah Okafor Achebe, was the teacher in charge of the Church Missionary Society's village school. Chinua Achebe attended this school and in 1944 went to Government College, Umuahia, in Eastern Nigeria. In 1953 he was one of the first students to graduate from the University College at Ibadan, then in special relation with the University of London. His formal studies in English literature would have been very similar to those of a British undergraduate. In those days the new British-style universities in Africa were intended to transplant on African soil what established academic circles in England regarded as the best features of English universities, without much regard for the special needs of the countries where they were set up.

In 1954 Achebe began a career in broadcasting as Talks Producer for the Nigerian Broadcasting Service, and in

1961 was appointed Director of External Broadcasting for Nigeria, an appointment which frequently took him abroad, to Britain and other parts of the world. He relinquished this post after the massacre of Ibos in Northern Nigeria in 1966 and moved back to the Eastern Region, where he was preparing to go into a new publishing venture with, among others, Christopher Okigbo. When the Eastern Region declared itself independent under the name of Biafra, Achebe threw in his lot with his fellow-Ibos.

In addition to the four novels discussed in this essay, Achebe has published some short stories in periodicals and *Chike and the River* (1966), a sixty-page children's story about a boy who realizes his ambition to cross the Niger by ferry and succeeds in exposing a gang of thieves.

III

Achebe's first novel, *Things Fall Apart*, was published in 1958. The title derives, of course, from W. B. Yeats's poem, 'The Second Coming', four lines of which are quoted on the title-page. In her article, 'Yeats and Achebe' in *The Journal of Commonwealth Literature*, No. 5 (1968), Miss A. G. Stock most persuasively argues the connection between the theme of *Things Fall Apart* and Yeats's vision of history as a succession of civilizations, each giving way to another through its own inability to embrace all human impulses satisfactorily within one enclosed order. She rightly emphasizes that Achebe is no mere disciple, but that he is using the Yeatsian idea as 'an instrument for analysing and interpreting' human experience in a confrontation between different ways of life.

It is a short and extraordinarily close-knit novel which in fictional terms creates the way of life of an Ibo village community when white missionaries and officials were first penetrating Eastern Nigeria. The highly selective details

with which Achebe represents the seasonal festivals and
ceremonies, the religion, social customs, and political
structure of an Ibo village create the vivid impression of a
complex, self-sufficient culture seemingly able to deal in
traditional ways with any challenge that nature and human
experience might fling at it. Many commentators have
stressed the 'charm' of this evocation of the African past, as
if Achebe's chief concern were to make a genuflection to
departed African glories, and show only that the coming of
the white man and his paraphernalia destroyed a finely-
wrought indigenous culture. Such a view is too limited. It
implies that Achebe has sentimentalized the setting of his
story, whereas the greatest strength of *Things Fall Apart* is
the tragic 'objectivity' with which Achebe handles a dual
theme.

There are two main, closely intertwined tragedies—the
personal tragedy of Okonkwo, 'one of the greatest men in
Umuofia', and the public tragedy of the eclipse of one
culture by another. The two are fused at the end, when
Okonkwo's ignominious death is shown to be part of a
greater fracturing: the once integrated, organic society of
Umuofia now shattered—its gods blasphemed, its customs
desecrated, the clan divided, a British District Commissioner in control. Yet in the course of the story
Okonkwo's motivations and actions have not all been
admirable, and the structure of Umuofia society has been
shown to have vulnerable cracks. Moreover, the first
Christian missionary is capable of common sense and fore-
bearance—it is his successor who is bigoted and helps to
bring on the catastrophe. In other words, although Achebe's
presentation of life in Umuofia is extremely sympathetic, it
is not totally idealized.

Okonkwo is a great man because he has assiduously
cultivated the energetic and aggressive qualities which tend
to be most admired in Umuofia. He began with nothing,
but by determination and hard work has won material
prosperity, the respect of his fellows, and a place among the

elders of the clan. It is he who is sent to the village of Mbaino as an emissary to deliver an ultimatum of war or the surrender of two hostages. On his return it is he who is entrusted with the care of Ikemefuna, the young male hostage, until the Oracle of the tribe should decide his fate. In his youth Okonkwo was the champion wrestler. Now he is a great warrior in a proud clan respected by all its neighbours because its Oracle never sends it out to do battle in an unjust cause. Here lies an important difference between Okonkwo's personal well-springs of action and those of the communal will of Umuofia, for in Okonkwo the desire to conquer and subdue is described as being 'like the desire for woman'. He rules his three wives and their children sternly, he knows 'how to kill a man's spirit', and yet not merely out of vindictiveness but because he expects in others the same iron exercise of self-discipline that he himself practised as a young man. Umuofia admires the solid achievements of this self-made man, though it wonders sometimes at his inability to show any emotion except anger. Okonkwo's personal dynamism has sprung from contempt for his improvident father, Unoka, a man who rejoiced in song, dance, and palm-wine, who preferred music to tending his yam fields. Unoka was always in debt, never took even the lowest title in the clan, and could not endure the sight of blood. The people tolerated though they despised him; they laughed at him while he lived and, because he 'died of the swelling which was an abomination to the earth goddess', he was left to die in the Evil Forest without ritual burial. With ruthless determination Okonkwo has gone to the other extreme of hating all that Unoka had loved, especially gentleness and idleness.

Okonkwo's tragedy lies in the price he pays for his lop-sided development as a person. Early on we are told: 'Perhaps down in his heart Okonkwo was not a cruel man', and various incidents hint at the effort it costs him to follow this corrosive ideal of conduct that he has set himself. His harshness towards his eldest son, Nwoye, arises out of a hungry impatience to see Nwoye become a strong man like himself, and out of fear that even the most legitimately boyish laziness exhibits symptoms of a temperament inherited from the grandfather. His hasty temper flares up and he beats his youngest wife during the Week of Peace; yet he submits quietly to the customary penalty of making a propitiatory offering at the shrine of the earth goddess. In fact he offers an additional pot of palm-wine and is inwardly genuinely repentant, but will not show it. This aloof silence about his own errors makes people wonder whether he respects the gods of the clan. Similarly, there is his heavy sigh of relief when he finds his favourite wife, Ekwefi, unhurt after he has fired at her in a fit of rage. Then, on the night when the priestess carries Ekwefi's daughter to the shrine in the hills for Agbala's blessing, and Ekwefi follows in terror for her child, Okonkwo surreptitiously follows her to be at hand when she needs re-assurance. As they wait together in the dawn Ekwefi remembers the generous love with which Okonkwo had taken her when she became his wife. For the reader, these rare revelations of Okonkwo's originally tender nature emphasize all the more the expense of spirit with which he usually damps down all outward signs of gentleness. Like Heyst in Joseph Conrad's *Victory*, Okonkwo has imposed a rigid code of aloofness upon his own generous human impulses and magnified it into a principle of right conduct.

This unnaturally stern and warping self-control extends beyond human relationships: Okonkwo can never relax, not even during clan festivals, like the feast of the New Yam, ordained by custom for thanksgiving to the earth goddess and recreation before the labours of harvest begin. Instead of joy, Okonkwo experiences only impatience with the enforced idleness.

Although he never shows it, Okonkwo grows fond of the young hostage, Ikemefuna, and the boy certainly comes to regard him as a father. After three years the Oracle suddenly declares that the time has come for Ikemefuna to be killed as tradition demands. Ogbuefi Ezeudu specifically warns Okonkwo to stay at home:

The Oracle of the Hills and the Caves has pronounced it. They will take him outside Umuofia as is the custom, and kill him there. But I warn you to have nothing to do with it. He calls you his father.

Those words, 'He calls you his father', indicate the flexibility and wisdom of the village culture that Achebe presents in this novel, and emphasize Okonkwo's limited understanding of what courage is. The gods of the clan may demand the sacrifice of Ikemefuna but they do not expect the members of the household where the victim has lived as a son to share in the ceremony. Even Okonkwo's closest friend, Obierika, feels absolved from participation because of his friendly links with the family. But precisely because Okonkwo feels love and pity for the boy, he fears that his manliness may be questioned, and so he accompanies the procession into the forest:

As the man who had cleared his throat drew up and raised his matchet, Okonkwo looked away. He heard the blow. The pot [of palm-wine] fell and broke in the sand. He heard Ikemefuna cry, 'My father, they have killed me!' as he ran towards him. Dazed with fear, Okonkwo drew his matchet and cut him down. He was afraid of being thought weak.

For two days Okonkwo eats nothing and tries to wash away the memory of that moment with palm-wine. He cannot sleep and only with a supreme effort of will does he conclude that this death was no different from those of the five men he has killed in battle. He resumes his normal activities and even tries to justify his action to Obierika. But the latter says: 'If I were you I would have stayed at home. What you have done will not please the Earth. It is the kind of action for which the goddess wipes out whole families.' Okonkwo simply cannot follow his friend's reasoning. In the same conversation we find him unable to comprehend how a former great warrior of Umuofia could have been so 'weak' as to do nothing without first telling his wife about it.

Later, at the funeral of Ogbuefi Ezeudu, Okonkwo's gun explodes and accidently kills Ezeudu's son. It is an unprecedented event, but even the inadvertent death of a clansman must be expiated, and so Okonkwo and his household have to flee before cockcrow, to endure seven years' exile. The next morning Okonkwo's compound is stormed and gutted in a ritual ceremony of 'cleansing the land which Okonkwo had polluted with the blood of a kinsman'.

When Okonkwo finds refuge with his mother's kinsfolk in the village of Mbanta, he has an opportunity to settle down in peace and work off the years of exile among generous, sympathetic people. But exile is gall to him—a disastrous break in his career of personal fulfilment just as he was ready to take the highest titles in his clan. He bends to the task of planting a new farm in Mbanta, but the zest of youth is gone; it's 'like learning to become left-handed in old age'. When he falls into a glowering despair his uncle tries to reason with him:

It's true that a child belongs to its father. But when a father beats his child, it seeks sympathy in its mother's hut. A man belongs to his fatherland when times are good and life is sweet. But when there is sorrow and bitterness he finds refuge in his motherland. Your mother is there to protect you. She is buried there. And that is why we say that mother is supreme.

Grateful as Okonkwo is for all the kindness he receives, he can only regard his time in Mbanta as a sojourn in the wilderness. He cannot see the wise balance in the tribal arrangements by which the female principle is felt to be simultaneously weak and sustaining. Moreover, during his exile he sees the people of Mbanta allowing the first Christian missionaries to establish a church, win adherents from among the outcasts of the village, and defy the powers of the tribal gods. His own son Nwoye, first estranged by Okonkwo's share in Ikemefuna's death, begins to attend Christian services in Mbanta, and, when Okonkwo tries to thrash him, leaves his father's compound and goes away to a mission school. Okonkwo urges the villagers to chase the 'abominable gang' of Christians away with whips. When they do not, he sighs afresh for his fatherland 'where men were bold and warlike'.

Like many another exile, Okonkwo thinks he is returning to the same fatherland he had left. But here too the Christians have built a church and attracted not only the low-born and outcast but even men of title. And with the missionaries has come white government—there is now a courthouse in Umuofia which lays down white law and has hanged a man whom traditional law would only have banished. As Obierika explains:

The white man is very clever. He came quietly and peaceably with his religion. We were amused at his foolishness and allowed him to stay. Now he has won our brothers, and our clan can no longer act as one. He has put a knife on the things that held us together and we have fallen apart.

So Okonkwo's return is neither the triumph he has dreamed of in exile nor is it a return to the warlike Umuofia he had known: men have become soft like women.

The climax is reached during a ceremony in honour of the earth goddess, when one of the more zealous converts (formerly held in check by the first missionary) tears the mask off one of the *egwugwu*, or masked spirits, who represent the ancestors of the clan. This is the ultimate desecration—an ancestral spirit has been killed. Next day the *egwugwu* advance on the Christian church and destroy it, for it 'has bred untold abominations'. Government intervenes, the elders are arrested and humiliated, the village is fined, and when a court messenger tries to stop a meeting of the clan, Okonkwo cuts him down. But he acts alone; the leaders of Umuofia are too divided to follow Okonkwo's warlike example, and so he goes and hangs himself. At the end Obierika turns to the District Commissioner and says ferociously: 'That man was one of the greatest men in Umuofia. You drove him to kill himself; and now he will be buried like a dog . . .'

This account of Okonkwo's career has tried to demonstrate that, despite the pathos of his ignominious death, Achebe's hero is portrayed as a man whose weaknesses are the obverse of his virtues. The failings are not glossed over, and Achebe implies throughout that Okonkwo is no mere automative victim of a social setting which encourages the qualities he has cultivated. He does have the power of choice; men as highly regarded as he for courage and strength of character are shown not to have expunged gentleness from their hearts. Umuofia may place less value on these gentler virtues but does acknowledge and provide for them. Nor is Okonkwo simply a victim of history. The District Commissioner may relegate his story to a single paragraph in the book he is planning on the *Pacification of the Primitive Tribes of the Lower Niger*, but Okonkwo's fall has been seen to be also the inevitable outcome of his own self-forged steeling of the gentler impulses.

The other tragic aspect of *Things Fall Apart* grows out of the conflict of cultures. The language of the people of Umuofia is full of Ibo proverbs (which Achebe renders into English) that allow well-tested traditional wisdom to be applied to problems of the present. If the nub of a contemporary situation can be seen to correspond to the generalized truth contained in a proverb, then present perplexity and past experience are made congruent, and language remains an effective instrument for coping with life. When Obierika grumbles indulgently that his son is always in too much of a hurry, he is reminded that he was also like that as a boy, and the speaker continues: 'As our people say, "When mother-cow is chewing grass its young ones watch its mouth". Maduka has been watching your mouth.' The proverb clinches the matter: no more need be

said. Much of the vividness with which the functioning of
Umuofia society is conveyed comes from Achebe's use of
these Ibo proverbs—like deft, sinewy brushstrokes they
reveal the clan's dependence upon traditional wisdom
transmitted linguistically, and thus lead us to apprehend a
whole way of life. The predictability of experience, thus
controlled by language, is augmented by the elaborate
rituals that mark the passing of the seasons and the important
events of a man's life—initiation, arrangement of bride-
price, marriage, war, litigation, burial. Very little of this
ceremonial is *explained*. Achebe brings it to life and
demonstrates its meaning by presenting events and con-
versations dramatically. What at first seem digressions from
the story of Okonkwo gradually become a progressive
creation of the daily lives of Okonkwo and the clan. The
impression emerges of a carefully ordered yet flexible
culture, communal in nature yet allowing for a considerable
measure of individuality. But not quite flexible enough to
survive the appearance of white men, something beyond
the reach of traditional knowledge. There is a limit to what
traditional experience can cope with: in Umuofia the term
'white man' has simply been a euphemism for 'leper'.

In important matters the clan has been accustomed to
respond as one organic entity, yet it has never been able to
enfold *all* its members. There have always been *osu*, or
outcasts, in a limbo existence with the clan but not of it;
there have always been unpopular wives who produce
twins. Among such people the seeds of Christian teaching
first sprout. Achebe seems to imply that Christianity is not
simply destructive of the old order, for its earliest adherents
are those whom the conventions of that order cannot
comfortably accommodate. The best example is Okonkwo's
gentle son, Nwoye, who reacts against his father's harshness
and warms to the Christian teaching of love. Though
Nwoye's desertion brings his father's curse upon him,
Nwoye is no monster of betrayal, any more than Okonkwo
is a heathen ruffian. Despite the Christian absorption of

Umuofia's misfits, the clan does try at first to come to uneasy terms with the new religion, thus enabling the inherent flaws in Umuofia society to develop into deep rifts that divide the clan against itself.

When the totally unprecedented happens there are no proverbs or rituals to guide the people. The explosion of Okonkwo's gun is such an event and it makes even so staunch a man as Obierika wonder why anyone should be punished so severely for an inadvertent 'offence'. He even questions what could possibly have been criminal about his wife's giving birth to twins. Unreasonable as he thinks these things, he nevertheless accepts them as the will of the earth goddess. When the Christians rescue twins abandoned in the Evil Forest, the clan are forced into the expedient of merely relying upon the letter of the old law. As long as the twins are not brought into the actual village, the clan pretend that they are still where they were left. When a Christian kills the sacred python, the clan again acquiesces, partly because of the tradition that the gods fight their own battles, but also out of sheer bewilderment—so unthinkable is the outrage that the forefathers never prescribed a penalty for the deliberate killing of a python. Similarly, when the *ogwugwu* is unmasked, there is no traditional punishment that can be enforced. When the elders do decide to destroy the Christian 'shrine', they show great tolerance towards the tactless missionary. They intend to curb his influence but are willing to allow him to stay and worship his own god, for they think it right that 'a man should worship the gods and the spirits of his fathers'. But, though admirable, this forbearance is fatal to the old religion, for the clansmen fail to understand the close links between the white priest and the white official. Thus the sacking of the church brings upon the elders the humiliation of arrest, imprisonment, and a communal fine. Disunity through defection, and now fear of the white official's power, thwart Okonkwo's hope that by killing the messenger he can spark off decisive communal action against the white intruders. He hangs himself, not to avoid arrest but out of despair for the future of his people. Then they too sense that there has been an irrevocable break with the past, that Umuofia can never again be what it was.

Things Fall Apart is impressive for the wide range of what it so pithily covers, for the African flavour of scene and language, but above all for the way in which Achebe makes that language the instrument for analyzing tragic experience and profound human issues of very much more than local Nigerian significance.

IV

Achebe's second novel, *No Longer at Ease*, was published in 1960. Again the title is taken from an English poet whose work explores the nature of civilization and the quality of twentieth-century life, this time from T. S. Eliot's poem, 'The Journey of the Magi'.

No Longer at Ease can be read, of course, simply as a sequel to *Things Fall Apart*, though to do so will excite expectations that Achebe has no intention of fulfilling. Obi, the chief character, is Okonkwo's grandson; his father is Okonkwo's son Nwoye, now a retired catechist living in Umuofia. Superficially *No Longer at Ease* seems merely to carry the themes of the other novel into the 1950s, but the differences of approach and treatment should warn against pressing the outward resemblances too far. Its austere contemporaneity, its insistence upon the ordinariness of a young man's failure to live up to his untried ideals of conduct, allow for none of the glamour that many readers have found in *Things Fall Apart*. A charge of bleakness cannot legitimately be brought against *No Longer at Ease*, for the greyer tones are essential to what seems to be Achebe's concern in this book. The reasons for one's sense that it is a lesser work must be sought elsewhere.

Umuofian society still represents values of the past, while the Nigerian capital, Lagos, is the cosmopolitan urban present, where everyone competes, no holds barred, for the meagre perks of incipient affluence. Umuofia is rurally conservative, a hybrid amalgam of pagan and established Christian respectabilities. It still clings to the notion of the ineradicable bonds of clan kinship, and though the liberal-ized Obi finds these suffocating, the concept does have some value in a confused, disruptive period of rapid change. Umuofians in Lagos may stand together rather flamboyantly (often absurdly) as the Umuofia Progressive Union, but they do help fellow-Umuofians in need. The eight-hundred-pound loan that sent Obi to the University of London was subscribed with real sacrifice by members of the Union. While Umuofians pontificate at their meetings in the cliché-ridden English of the popular press and render thanks to 'the Man Above', they still quote traditional Ibo proverbs at one another. The humblest, least-educated speak Ibo to fellow-Umuofians, otherwise Pidgin. The educated speak English of varying degrees of formality, and break into Pidgin when they wish to sound friendly. When Obi addresses the UPU after his return from England, he begins in a patriotic burst of Ibo but gradually settles into the English he is more familiar with. The anglicized cabinet minister reverts to Pidgin when he feels expansive among a few friends. These carefully recorded language habits contribute much to the sense of flux and uncertainty that the Lagos scenes generate.

But Achebe does not merely record. Though he exposes the slums behind the tinsel glitter of Lagos, though he contrasts humbug and official corruption with the energetic warmth of ordinary life in the city, he does not offer Umuofia as a valid alternative. On the contrary, despite the humane virtues that still shelter beneath Umuofian solid-arity, Achebe more often than not presents the Lagos Umuofians satirically. As in *Things Fall Apart*, we hear again the clan salute *Umuofia Kwenu!* and the choral response *Ya!*, but from the throats of the Umuofia Progressive Union it rings like a comic mockery of the formal opening of a clan assembly that used to thunder across the market place. The UPU has turned Obi into Umuofia's first graduate, and thus into the new Secretary of the government Scholarship Board. Obi becomes Umuofia's 'only palm fruit' in the upper echelons of the civil service, and he is looked to for the influence he will exert on behalf of Umuofians anxious for some crumbs from the national cake, or, as they put it: 'Shall we kill a snake and carry it in our hand, when we have a bag for putting long things in?' In dealing with the contemporary scene, Achebe's clear mind and sensitivity to nuances have been unable to pass over absurdities in human behaviour that he has probably witnessed, but the question is whether this has happened more frequently than his ultimate intentions in *No Longer at Ease* warrant. The treatment of the few Europeans who figure in the novel is justifiably satirical, for Achebe naturally sees them from the receiving end of colonialism in Africa. Thus, in Obi's child-hood, for a Nigerian teacher to throw an arrogant white inspector to the floor is likened to unmasking an ancestral spirit—a superbly ironic reversal of the climactic unmasking in *Things Fall Apart*. What is stressed about Obi's superior, Mr Green, is his paternalism and contempt for Nigerians, yet Achebe does also understand the near-tragic situation of white men wanting 'to bring light to the heart of darkness' and being overwhelmed not by Kurtz's darkness but by the 'incipient dawn', as Obi puts it.

Nevertheless, *No Longer at Ease* seems to be too socially satirical to be able to carry off convincingly the tragic effect Achebe gives us reason to think he is striving for. What one misses is the artistically cohesive tension between chief character and setting that occurs in *Things Fall Apart*. The setting is as economically and convincingly created, but is felt to be almost incidental to the story of Obi. Like one of the magi, Obi returns from abroad, having caught the flavour of a different—an efficient, rational—dispensation. His mind is packed full of elevated notions of public service, and he is determined to play his full part in reinvigorating the Nigerian civil service and stamping out all the old corruption that so ill befits a new nation. The story records his failure. It is an attempt at a tale of muted tragedy, told laconically rather than with detachment.

Achebe's method is clearly hinted at in the account of Obi's interview for his job. During a discussion of Graham Greene's *The Heart of the Matter*, Obi says that life is 'like a bowl of wormwood which one sips a little at a time world without end'. 'A real tragedy', he asserts, 'takes place in a corner, in an untidy spot.' It would seem that Achebe intends Obi's story to be tragic in this sort of Audenesque way, a view confirmed by the very banal level at which Obi's defeat takes place. He succumbs because loans have to be repaid, money sent home, expenses accounted for. For this effect to be produced Obi has to be made so naïve and self-deluded that he comes close to appearing merely childish. While his story can also be read partly as a paradigm of a man caught between the irreconcilable values of different ways of life, his enmeshment happens too easily to win our sympathetic involvement. As the catalogue of debts and expenditure mounts, one becomes too aware of the cards being stacked against him. It is a very simple-minded young man indeed who does not expect to receive a demand for income tax or an electricity bill.

This gormlessness of Obi's contradicts the intellectual ability he has for analyzing the augean state of Nigerian officialdom. Not that Achebe endows him with a powerful intellect—his gravest flaw is indeed a rather priggish romantic idealism, a tendency to react all too easily to the glib public sentiment and to inflated talk about public service. The absurd poem, 'Nigeria', that he wrote in London in the style of a nineteenth-century English hymn, is understandable as a young student's nostalgic effusion in a foreign city, but he smiles complacently when he comes across it in a melancholy mood after his first quarrel with Clara. His book of consolatory reading is A. E. Housman's *Collected Poems*. What Obi lacks is all power of self-analysis.

In times of personal crisis he either misses completely the really very obvious causes, or so mis-reads his motives that further disasters are inevitable. The laconic tone in which the author narrates the following passage illustrates how difficult it is for the reader to square the tragic implications of Obi's story with Achebe's refusal to give the character a chance:

The chief result of the crisis in Obi's life was that it made him examine critically for the first time the main-spring of his actions. And in doing so he uncovered a good deal that he could only regard as sheer humbug. Take this matter of twenty pounds every month to his town union, which in the final analysis was the root cause of all his troubles. Why had he not swallowed his pride and accepted the four months' exemption which he had been allowed, albeit with a bad grace? Could a person in his position afford that kind of pride? Was it not a common saying among his people that a man should not, out of pride and etiquette, swallow his phlegm?

Having seen the situation in its true light, Obi decided to stop payment forthwith until such time as he could do it conveniently.

Obi has a very romantic imagination—a seascape moves him 'deeply'; so does 'the wealth of association' in even a mediocre popular Ibo song; soon after his mother's death he is horrified to find that he can still eat and sleep. On the other hand, there is his love of Clara, whom he wants to marry, but even here Achebe maintains a too-violent dichotomy between Obi's intellectual and instinctual responses. When Clara tells him that they cannot marry because she is an *osu*, she is reminding him that despite their overseas education they are still under the shadow of the most firmly rooted of all Ibo taboos. Obi argues clearly, logically, in full accord with his own idea of himself as a rational 'new' man:

It was scandalous that in the middle of the twentieth century a man could be barred from marrying a girl simply because her great-great-great-great-grandfather had been dedicated to serve a god, thereby setting himself apart and turning his descendants into a forbidden caste to the end of time.

Yet what had been his immediate reaction when Clara told him?

'I am an *osu*,' she wept. Silence. She stopped weeping and quietly disengaged herself from him. Still he said nothing.

'So you see we cannot get married,' she said, quite firmly, almost gaily—a terrible kind of gaiety. Only the tears showed she had wept.

'Nonsense!' said Obi. He shouted it almost, as if by shouting it now he could wipe away those seconds of silence, when everything had seemed to stop, waiting in vain for him to speak.

From then on he tries to erase that betraying silence, speaking of the marriage as something assured and any opposition from his family as obstacles he will certainly overcome. When he goes home to Umuofia and his father declares very simply that he cannot marry the girl, the 'liberated' son speciously uses the very arguments against him that the catechist might himself use in talking to his heathen clansmen: 'Our fathers in their darkness and ignorance called an innocent man *osu* . . . But have we not seen the light of the Gospel?'

Obi's resolution is defeated when his ailing mother threatens to kill herself if he marries an *osu* in her lifetime, while his father tells him the story of Ikemefuna's death, and demolishes his pseudo-Christian arguments with these words:

I tell you all this so that you may know what it was in those days to become a Christian. I left my father's house, and he placed a curse on me. I went through fire to become a Christian. Because I suffered I understand Christianity—more than you will ever do.

He finds there is nothing in him that can challenge his parents' attitudes honestly. For all his pioneering stance he must go back to Clara and lamely suggest that they 'lie quiet for a little while'. But she reads the signs clearly and

knows that all is over. Not even the knowledge of her
pregnancy can inflame his former glib arguments into a
genuine belief. Only after Clara is driven away in the
doctor's car for the abortion to be performed does Obi
want to shout after her, 'Stop. Let's go and get married
now'. During her subsequent illness Clara simply rejects
him and passes out of his life.

Meanwhile, as his extravagant living since his return to
Nigeria demands payment, Obi's intellectually held princi-
ples about integrity in the civil service also give way. He
falsifies his travelling-expenses sheet and begins to accept
bribes for ensuring that applicants' names are placed on the
short list for scholarships. But about one thing he is un-
shakeable—he 'stoutly refused to countenance anyone who
did not possess the minimum educational and other require-
ments'. When the police set a trap with marked notes, he is
arrested, tried, found guilty. Obi as a listless, uninterested
prisoner in the dock, with his sensibility dulled, is the scene
with which the novel had opened. After all he has been
through, the only Umuofian with an overseas degree has
learned 'to look words like "education" and "promise"
squarely in the face'—with a cynic's smile and some in-
voluntary tears.

It will have been seen that though the structure of *No
Longer at Ease* is slighter, the wider issues that lie behind Obi's
failure are in themselves perhaps more complicated than
those so vividly raised in *Things Fall Apart*. This is another,
more legitimate, reason why Obi appears as a lost child
rather than a tragic figure.

V

With *Arrow of God*, published in 1964, Achebe returns to
the kind of society portrayed in *Things Fall Apart*, but one
must qualify the word 'returns' for, despite all the outward
resemblances of the two novels, *Arrow of God* is a new

development in Achebe's art. It is a different *kind* of novel:
not simply a study in greater depth of clan society, not simply
a more leisurely canvas less impressionistically executed.
The focus is now much less upon the clash of cultures in an
historical process, as upon the clash of rival personalities and
policies within the full spectrum of a clan's internal politics.
It is true that the presence of a mission church and school
in Umuaro is almost taken for granted, and that by 1921
even this remote clan has reason to know that Government
Hill exists at Okperi some distance away. To this extent the
things of the ancient dispensation have already fallen apart,
but though missionaries and white officials do influence the
course of events in Umuaro, they do so only as catalytic
agents acting upon a process generated by pressures within
Umuaro that go back to the origins of the clan, generations
before the coming of the white man. Captain Winterbottom, the District Officer at Okperi, is grossly ignorant
of tribal customs and beliefs, and remains to the end un-
aware of the outcome of the events in Umuaro in which he
once intervened personally and at other times from a
distance.

The central character of *Arrow of God* is Ezeulu, the clan's
Chief Priest who officiates for its protecting deity, Ulu.
There are frequent references to the distant past—to how
the six villages of Umuaro united as a clan in self-defence
against the warriors of Abam, and chose the priest of the
new clan god from the weakest of the villages so as to
forestall internal strife arising out of the importance of the
priestly office. The novel opens with Ezeulu scanning the
evening sky for the first sign of the new moon. When it
appears, his function is to announce its arrival, ceremonially
eat the next of the sacred yams that mark the passing
months, and calculate and proclaim to the clan the day for
the feast of the Pumpkin Leaves. The central issue of the
book is raised immediately:

Whenever Ezeulu considered the immensity of his power over the
year and the crops and, therefore, over the people he wondered if it was

real. It was true he named the day for the feast of the Pumpkin Leaves and for the New Yam feast; but he did not choose the day. He was merely a watchman. His power was no more than the power of a child over a goat that was said to be his. As long as the goat was alive it was his; he would find it food and take care of it. But the day it was slaughtered he would know who the real owner was. No! the Chief Priest of Ulu was more than that, must be more than that. If he should refuse to name the day there would be no festival—no planting and no reaping. But could he refuse? No Chief Priest had ever refused. So it could not be done. He would not dare.

Nothing seems very different from the past. Tradition has laid down and circumscribed each successive Chief Priest's powers, yet here is the priest (half man, half inscrutable spirit, as his closest friend observes later) meditating on the difference between his aspiring human sense of power as the clan's Chief Priest, and the seemingly mechanical, limited nature of the exercise of that power. The trend of Ezeulu's thoughts arises out of the war with the Okperi clan five years before, when Umuaro had not heeded his counsel. The dispute had been over some land claimed by both clans, and Ezeulu had tried to dissuade Umuaro from war on the grounds that their cause was not clear-cut and their fathers had never fought 'a war of blame'. But Nwaka, one of the three highest-titled men of Umuaro, had won general support, and for the first time Umuaro went to war divided. The District Officer had intervened and Ezeulu had won his respect by being the only man on both sides who seemed to speak the truth irrespective of clan loyalty. In consequence officialdom awarded the land to Okperi, with two far-reaching political consequences in Umuaro. On the one hand, Nwaka and Ezidemili (priest of the village god Idemili), both ambitious men belonging to the strongest of the six villages, begin to represent Ezeulu as a friend of the white man and as priest of the relatively upstart god, Ulu, whose 'creation' dates only from the unification of the villages, whereas the original village deities existed long before. On the other hand, Ezeulu sees

the unhappy outcome of the war as justifying his warning
against it. But Ezeulu has also been greatly impressed by
Captain Winterbottom's power. The white man had not
only stopped the war but broken the clan's guns. Ezeulu's
duty, on behalf of the protecting deity whose priest he is, is
to divine the future and take what measures he can for the
clan's safety. The future now involves a previously unknown
power, whose secret needs to be penetrated. Ezeulu's
solution was to make what amounted to a great personal
sacrifice for one who embodied the most sacred traditions
of Umuaro. He sent his son Oduche to the mission school:

'The world is changing,' he had told him. 'I do not like it. But I am like
the bird Eneke-nti-oba. When his friends asked him why he was always
on the wing he replied: "Men of today have learnt to shoot without
missing and so I have learnt to fly without perching." I want one of my
sons to join these people and be my eye there. If there is nothing in it
you will come back. But if there is something there you will bring home
my share. The world is like a Mask dancing. If you want to see it well
you do not stand in one place. My spirit tells me that those who do not
befriend the white man today will be saying *had we known* tomorrow.'

But are Ezeulu's motives disinterested, entirely on behalf
of his people's future? Is he more wise and adaptable than
his fellows? Or does he wish to learn the secrets of white
power in order to enhance his own, now questioned,
influence within Umuaro? This is the real theme of *Arrow
of God*. It is never explicitly elucidated, for Achebe allows
us to see only a little further into Ezeulu's mind than the
clan does. In the end they are persuaded by Nwaka and
Ezidemili that Ezeulu wants to be 'king, priest, diviner, all'.
Ezeulu is too proud to explain himself clearly, and so while
his actions are left to speak largely for themselves, they speak
with a tragically enigmatic ambiguity. The opposition are
able to interpret all his words and actions against him: thus
Oduche's being sent to the mission school is merely further
evidence of Ezeulu's dangerous friendship with the white
man. Whatever Ezeulu's actual motives may be, he sees

himself always as acting by proxy first for the god Ulu and then for the clan. This is no mere delusion of grandeur, though ideally his office demands that the interests of god and clan should coincide. As they gain ground his enemies, of course, increasingly argue that Ulu's power may be questioned in proportion to their success in discrediting Ezeulu.

This is Achebe's most ambitious piece of characterization yet, and it is done with the same power of subtle analytic ordering that went into the representation of the clash of cultures in *Things Fall Apart*. Ezeulu becomes a truly tragic figure, proud, aloof, dedicated to his office, yet aspiring beyond its limitations for what he believes is the future safety of his people, and later, when the crisis is reached, for what he convinces himself is the true dignity of his god. That the other characters as well as the reader can interpret his motives as those of personal arrogance makes that tragedy of the same ironic kind as Macbeth's defiling his mind that 'Banquo's issue' may be kings.

When Winterbottom peremptorily summons Ezeulu to Okperi, without explanation but in fact to make him Paramount Chief of Umuaro, Ezeulu's sense of his own and his people's dignity is so outraged that he refuses to go and is eventually escorted there under arrest. It is at this stage that he gives the assembly of Umuaro elders their last chance to do proper homage to Ulu. Again they are persuaded by Nwaka, on grounds which ironically go back to the very measures that Ezeulu has taken to equip the clan for meeting the white man's power. So Ezeulu goes to Okperi alone, without the moral support of his people. His detention on Government Hill means that two new moons go unannounced in Umuaro; nor can Ezeulu eat the sacred monthly yams that mark the passing year.

After his return home he in effect prolongs the natural year by two months, by refusing to eat more than one yam at the next new moon. Thus the feast of the New Yam, without which the harvest cannot be gathered, is delayed.

Hunger and suffering follow, while the yam harvest rots in the ground. But Ezeulu sees himself as the arrow of his god piercing the heart of Umuaro for its disrespect towards Ulu and his priest. Here the implication does seem to be that Ezeulu's arrogance has ironically caused him to reverse the very function of his office—to bring deliberate disaster upon the people instead of averting it. When his son Obika collapses and dies in a ritual ceremony, the people take it as Ulu's punishment on Ezeulu for his presumption. In the anguish of personal loss and public humiliation his mind cracks and he lives his last days 'in the haughty splendour of a demented high priest', thus spared, however, all knowledge of the final outcome. The people conclude that their god has upheld 'the wisdom of their ancestors—that no man however great was greater than his people', but the final paragraph of the novel qualifies so facile an interpretation of Ezeulu's career by placing it within a larger and even more ironic context:

If this was so then Ulu had chosen a dangerous time to uphold this wisdom. In destroying his priest he had also brought disaster on himself, like the lizard in the fable who ruined his mother's funeral by his own hand. For a deity who chose a time such as this to destroy his priest or abandon him to his enemies was inciting people to take liberties; and Umuaro was just ripe to do so. The Christian harvest which took place a few days after Obika's death saw more people than even Good-country [the catechist] could have dreamed. In his extremity many an Umuaro man had sent his son with a yam or two to offer to the new religion and to bring back the promised immunity. Thereafter any yam that was harvested in the man's fields was harvested in the name of the son.

In *Arrow of God* there is the same kind of traditionalism expressed through Ibo proverbs as in *Things Fall Apart*, but the linguistic texture is richer and there is a new dimension in the use of the proverbs. The fuller scale on which the novel is conceived allows for greater elaboration in the descriptions of ceremonies as well as domestic life and personal relations, for instance the colourful account of Ezeulu's role as absolver of the clan's sins in the great feast of the Pumpkin Leaves. This is not just a decoration; it is necessary for an adequate understanding of Ezeulu and his relationship with the people. The proverbs are also used as one means of conveying what is essential for the literary realization of Ezeulu's particular situation—that he is part man, part spirit in the minds of the people. In the description of the 'priesting' of Ezeulu's ancestor, the first Chief Priest, and even more so in the account of Obika's ritual impersonization of the spirit Ogbazulobodo, Achebe uses passages that consist entirely of a succession of proverbs passing through the character's mind. The incantatory effect creates most vividly the sense of a single human being taking upon himself the timeless identity of the spirit he has for the moment become.

In *Arrow of God* Achebe has clearly returned to the African past with relish and a new confidence in his ability to evoke a way of life with which the legends of his childhood had familiarized him. He has himself said that one reason for his interest in the past is to help his fellow-Africans to a real pride in their own, pre-colonial culture. These were his words at a conference in Leeds in 1964:

. . . it would be foolish to pretend that we have fully recovered from the traumatic effects of our first confrontation with Europe. Three or four weeks ago my wife who teaches English in a boys' school asked a pupil why he wrote about winter when he meant the harmattan. He said he would be laughed out of class if he did such a thing! Now, you wouldn't have thought, would you, that there was something shameful in your weather? But apparently we do. How can this great blasphemy be purged? I think it is part of my business as a writer to teach that boy that there is nothing disgraceful about the African weather, that the palm-tree is a fit subject for poetry . . .

I would be quite satisfied if my novels (especially the ones I set in the past) did no more than teach my readers that their past—with all its imperfections—was not one long night of savagery from which the first Europeans acting on God's behalf delivered them. Perhaps what I write is applied art as distinct from pure. But who cares? Art is important but so is education of the kind I have in mind. And I don't see that the two need be mutually exclusive.

(*Commonwealth Literature*, ed. J. Press, London, 1965, pp. 204-5.)

But another, perhaps unconscious, reason becomes manifest when one compares his two 'African past' with his two 'contemporary' novels. In *No Longer at Ease* he is unable to avoid a satirical tone; *A Man of the People* is entirely, bitterly satirical. Achebe would seem to find it more congenial to achieve the detachment essential for a tragic work when he can set it not in the present that he is physically involved in, but in the past—though not the past that the term 'historical novel' suggests. Rather a past that was still authentically transmitted by word of mouth when he was young, and was still so alive in the language of Ibo legend and everyday speech that he could acquire a real inwardness with its subtleties and nuances.

VI

A Man of the People (1966) certainly demonstrates that Achebe's strength is not limited to dealing with the Africa of the past. Some reviewers greeted it as an entirely new departure in Achebe's writing, but in the first place it is a development of the urban themes already present in *No Longer at Ease*, and secondly, the overall treatment of the chief character within a carefully constructed and fully realized social and political setting is the sort of undertaking that, for all their differences, the preceding novels have led us to expect.

Nevertheless, *A Man of the People* is a very different kind of novel—a satirical farce about corrupt politicians cynically exploiting a political system inherited from the departed imperial power. So disillusioned is the *exposé* that the author would hardly seem to escape a charge of personal cynicism. None of the characters is admirable, and the one concession to any sort of faith in human behaviour is in a very low key. At the end Odili, the chief character and narrator, sums up his attitude to the whole political situation that the novel has explored:

... in such a regime, I say, you died a good death if your life had inspired someone to come forward and shoot your murderer in the chest— without asking to be paid.

These are the last words in the book, and unless Odili's double function as narrator and 'anti-hero' is kept constantly in mind, it would be all too easy to confuse the character's sentiments with the author's. In this novel Achebe doesn't comment: the method is even more fully dramatic than it was in *Arrow of God*. He places Odili on the stage and leaves him there both to perform in and to comment on the action, so that everything is filtered through his consciousness, but the language that Odili uses is a constant reminder that we cannot take him at face value.

Though with many modulations, Odili speaks throughout in the *blasé*, sophisticated tone of a young man who prides himself on being able to see even the depraved in human behaviour as merely laughable. He has the slickness of phrase, the glibness of gibe, the superiority of smugness, that one associates with many a television personality. Here he reflects on the climax of his political adventuring:

The events of the next four weeks or so have become so widely known in the world at large that there would be little point in my relating them in any detail here. And in any case, while those events were happening I was having a few private problems of my own. My cracked cranium took a little time to mend—to say nothing of the broken arm and countless severe bruises one of which all but turned me into a kind of genealogical cul-de-sac.

Yet at the same time he is so taken in by his performance that he is for ever deluding himself and appears to be dis-armingly innocent. Achebe uses this side of Odili's character skilfully, as a Gulliver-like means of obtaining some of his most telling satiric effects against the political life of post-Independence Nigeria. Odili, the young graduate school-master who challenges a corrupt cabinet minister at the polls, would have us believe in his crusading role, but his un-convincing, vaguely leftish political stance is only a hastily donned disguise to cover his real motive—personal revenge against Chief the Hon. M. A. Nanga, who has outwitted him in an amatory intrigue. It is a brilliant conception. Achebe can use Odili to lay bare bribery, the efficient pursuit of self-interest, and national apostasy on a thorough-going scale; simultaneously the very transparency of Odili's real motives and his blindness to their implications under-mine constantly the impression he tries to give of his own integrity. His actions show him to be different from the corrupt professionals only in being less practised in the ways of chicanery, bribery and thuggery. The new political party that supports him is potentially as crooked in its methods as the longer-established POP and PAP, its leaders quite as hypocritical.

On the political side Odili's empty pretentions are mercilessly revealed when the simple 'bush' woman, Edna's mother, dismisses both him and Chief Nanga in the same breath: 'They are both white man's people. And they know what is what between themselves. What do we know?' But Odili is fighting on another front as well, trying to win from Nanga the attractive Edna, who is about to become the Chief's second wife. His seemingly real love of her is also shown to be a spurious emotion. He thrills ridiculously to the letter Edna sends him, which begins: 'Your missive of 10th instant was received . . .' and ends:

I hope we will always be friends. For yesterday is but a dream and tomorrow is only a vision but today's friendship makes every yesterday a dream of happiness and every tomorrow a vision of hope.

Although Odili recognizes some phrases that could only have come from a popular handbook like *The Complete*

Love-letter Writer, he tries, not very successfully, to discern signs in the writing of 'her sweet spontaneous self'. Nevertheless he feels greatly encouraged and flutters emotionally to the hotch-potch of cliché and false sentiment, especially the phrase 'sweet dreams'. This incident sets up linguistic tones which call in question the whole relationship between Odili and Edna, with its happy ending.

One disadvantage of separating Achebe's four novels into those set in the African past and those in contemporary Nigeria is that it tends to obscure the confident mastery over a wide range of speech and language usage, the close interaction between language and theme that is common to all his novels. It is chiefly through their own manipulation of language that the politicians in *A Man of the People* condemn themselves. Their crude anti-intellectualism finds expression in the thoughtless flow of platform rhetoric with which they attain a meretricious eloquence in English:

'Owner of book!' cried one admirer, assigning in those three brief words the ownership of the white man's language to the Honourable Minister, who turned round and beamed on the speaker.

Sometimes they adapt traditional proverbs in clumsy attempts to justify a system of graft and injustice, as when a poor man is rebuked for envying a minister's income:

My people get one proverb: they say that when poor man done see with him own eye how to make big man e go beg make e carry him poverty de go je-je.

One difficulty that *A Man of the People* presents to the non-West African reader is the frequent use of Pidgin in the dialogue. It does, however, make for authenticity, and one gradually learns to follow most of its grammar and syntax.

There is some contrast made between urban and village life, though Achebe can find no village light with which to cheer the dense political gloom. All that emerges is that small unurbanized communities still possess some traditional means of coping with public outrage. Josiah, a shopkeeper who cheats a blind beggar, is boycotted and has to leave the village because the people realize that he has now gone too far—he 'has taken away enough for the owner to notice'. An Ibo proverb indicates that in a village, at any rate, public wrongs can be set right through effective communal action fired by spontaneous recognition that the experience of the forefathers preserved in the language of the present can still have meaning. Moreover, Odili, with his western style education, is estranged from such a communal sense of moral values, which in his view has no continuing validity. He completely misunderstands his father's ways, a man by no means free of faults who is nevertheless still in tenuous touch with some of the more admirable values of the past. Only once, and very fleetingly, does Odili wonder whether he has 'got everything terribly, lopsidedly wrong'. He even wonders why public action at village level cannot be transmuted into public action at national level.

The book insists that the corrupt politicians have so inured public opinion to the existing state of affairs that ordinary people have lapsed into despairing resignation:

As he gave instance after instance of how some of our leaders who were ash-mouthed paupers five years ago had become near-millionaires under our very eyes, many of the audience laughed. But it was the laughter of resignation to misfortune. No one among them swore vengeance; no one shook with rage or showed any sign of fight. They understood what was being said, they had seen it with their own eyes. But what did anyone expect them to do?

A Man of the People is a sparkling piece of satirical virtuosity, yet we feel throughout that deep anger, bitterness and disillusion are never far beneath the surface. The novel prompts one to ask: Is it too savage, too despairing, too Swiftian? Many readers find it so, but the skill with which Odili's dual function is controlled and the hints at other criteria of judgement (in Edna's mother's remark and the village action against Josiah) do pose values other than those of the 'eat-and-let-eat' politicians. In including a military *coup* as the climax to the political chaos, Achebe is far from suggesting a practical remedy, for he treats it simply as another self-interested action in the larger national 'game'; the *coup* happens because there was 'so much unrest and dislocation that our young Army officers seized the opportunity to take over'. The people remain lethargic and cynical. A satirist is under no obligation to offer a blue-print for political action, and Achebe has been content in *A Man of the People* to rub his reader's noses in the unsavoury details of public offence set in Nigeria but familiar in many other countries as well.

Since the outbreak of the Nigeria-Biafra war Chinua Achebe has been living in war-torn Biafra, where he has been undertaking official work for the Biafran authorities, including missions abroad. While he was in Uganda in 1968 helping to prepare the way for the Kampala peace talks that broke down, he was interviewed by a representative of *Transition*. A transcript of the interview appears in *Transition*, No. 36 (July 1968). From it one learns of his commitment to what he sees as 'a fundamental cause' which trancends ordinary politics. He has witnessed many of the horrors of war, had had his home destroyed by bombing, has had to learn to live with 'horrible things' that form a normal part of a strange, new kind of life. When the war began he was working on a new novel:

In fact, I was writing something which suddenly seemed irrelevant to me. What seemed important to me at the time as a subject matter for a novel seemed unimportant compared with what was happening, and also I think even if I felt like seeing my way through to a brilliant novel, I might, in fact, not find the emotional or even the physical convenience to do it. I have tried to do little things, like poems.

Whatever the outcome of the war, one can only hope fervently that a novelist who is so conscious and gifted a literary artist as Achebe has proved himself to be will survive the fighting and be able to resume his writing career; and that the Ibo people, whose strengths and weaknesses, whose vitality and pride are celebrated in his novels, will soon be able to contribute their creative skills once more to the common heritage of human arts.

CHINUA ACHEBE

A Select Bibliography

(Books published in London unless stated otherwise)

Collected Works:

THE SACRIFICIAL EGG AND OTHER STORIES; Onitsha, Nigeria (1962)
—five stories written between 1952 and 1960 with brief introduction by M. T. C. Echerno.

Separate Works:

THINGS FALL APART, (1958). *Novel*
'The Sacrificial Egg', *Atlantic Monthly*, April 1959; New York. *Short Story*.
NO LONGER AT EASE (1960). *Novel*
ARROW OF GOD (1964). *Novel*
'The Voter', *Black Orpheus*, 17, 1965; Ikeja, Nigeria
A MAN OF THE PEOPLE (1966). *Novel*
CHIKE AND THE RIVER (1966).
—a short novel for children.

Articles:

'Where Angels Fear to Tread', *Nigeria Magazine*, 75, 1962; Lagos
—an article on European and American critics of Nigerian authors.
'On Janheinz Jahn and Ezekiel Mphahlele', *Transition*, 8, 1963; Kampala, Uganda
—on theories about African literature.
'The Role of the Writer in a New Nation', *Nigeria Magazine*, 81, 1964; Lagos
—about the need for new African writers to undertake 'a spiritual search' for their roots.
'Conversation with Chinua Achebe', by Lewis Nkosi, *Africa Report*, IX, vii, 1964, African American Institute; Washington, DC
—a transcript of an interview with Achebe.
COMMONWEALTH LITERATURE, ed. John Press, (1965)
—contains 'The Novelist as Teacher', text of Achebe's address to Conference on Commonwealth literature, Leeds, 1964.
A SELECTION OF AFRICAN PROSE, ed. W. H. Whiteley, I: *Traditional Oral Texts;* Oxford (1964)
—contains 'Foreword' by Achebe.

'English and the African Writer', *Transition*, 18, 1965; Kampala, Uganda.

'The Burden of the Negro Writer', *Présence Africaine*, 59, 1966; Paris.

'Chinua Achebe Interviewed by Robert Serumaga', *Cultural Events in Africa*, 28, 1967; The Transcription Centre
—a transcript of a recorded interview with Achebe.

'Chinua Achebe on Biafra', *Transition*, 36, 1968; Kampala, Uganda
—transcript of an interview in Kampala.

Some Critical Studies:

SEVEN AFRICAN WRITERS, by G. Moore (1962)
—contains chapter entitled 'Chinua Achebe: Nostalgia and Realism', dealing with *Things Fall Apart* and *No Longer at Ease*.

'Achebe's New Novel', by Gerald Moore, *Transition* 14, 1964; Kampala, Uganda
—a review of *Arrow of God*.

'Language and Theme in *Things Fall Apart*', by E. D. Jones, *A Review Of English Literature*, V, iv, 1964.

'The Language of African Literature', by E. Mphahlele, *Harvard Educational Review;* XXXIV, ii, 1964; Cambridge, Mass., USA
—includes discussion of Achebe's work.

'The Offended *Chi* in Achebe's Novels', by A. J. Shelton, *Transition*, 13, 1964; Kampala, Uganda
—on *Things Fall Apart* and *No Longer at Ease*.

AFRICAN/ENGLISH LITERATURE, by A. Tibble (1965)
—an anthology with an Introduction which includes discussion of Achebe's novels.

THE GLORY AND THE GOOD: ESSAYS IN LITERATURE, by P. Nandakumar; New Delhi, (1965)
—contains chapter entitled 'Chinua Achebe'.

'English Words, African Lives', by G. Moore, *Présence Africaine*, 54, 1965; Paris
—No. 26 in English edition.

'Nigerian Prose Literature in English', by J. Ferguson, *English Studies in Africa*, VIII, ii, 1965; Witwatersrand University Press, Johannesburg
—includes discussion of *Things Fall Apart*.

'Out of the Irony of Words', by J. Gleason, *Transition*, 18, 1965; Kampala, Uganda
—includes discussion of Achebe's work.

'Recent African Fiction', by D. Killam, *The Bulletin of the Association for African Literature in English*, 2, 1966; Fourah Bay College, Freetown, Sierra Leone

—includes discussion of *Arrow of God*.

'The Clashing Old and New', by R. Green, *The Nation*, CCI, 11, 1965; New York

—includes Achebe in discussion of how African writers deal with current issues in Africa.

'Odili's Progress', *Times Literary Supplement*, 3 February 1966;

—a review of *A Man of the People*.

AN INTRODUCTION TO WEST AFRICAN LITERATURE, by Oladele Taiwo (1967)

—contains chapter entitled 'Chinua Achebe, *No Longer at Ease*', a schoolmasterly analysis of the novel.

'The Legacy of Caliban', by J. P. Clark, *Black Orpheus*, II, i, 1968; Mbari, Ibadan, Nigeria

—includes discussion of Achebe's use of language.

'The Palm Oil with which Achebe's Words are Eaten', by B. Lindfors, *African Literature Today*, 1, 1968

—discusses the language, and especially the imagery, of the novels.

LONG DRUMS AND CANNONS: NIGERIAN DRAMATISTS AND NOVELISTS 1952-1966, by M. Laurence (1968)

—contains chapter entitled 'The Thickets of our Separateness', a full treatment of Achebe's novels.

'Yeats and Achebe', by A. G. Stock, *The Journal of Commonwealth Literature*, 5, 1968

—deals mainly with *Things Fall Apart*.

'African Literature V: Novels of Disillusion', by A. Ravenscroft, *The Journal of Commonwealth Literature*, 6, 1969

—includes discussion of *A Man of the People*.

WHISPERS FROM A CONTINENT: THE LITERATURE OF CONTEMPORARY BLACK AFRICA, by W. Cartey; New York (1969)

—includes discussion of Achebe's novels.

Note: *My grateful thanks are due to Professor Douglas Killam of York University, Toronto, for help in compiling this bibliography.*

WRITERS AND THEIR WORK

General Surveys:

THE DETECTIVE STORY IN BRITAIN:
Julian Symons

THE ENGLISH BIBLE: Donald Coggan

ENGLISH VERSE EPIGRAM:
G. Rostrevor Hamilton

ENGLISH HYMNS: A. Pollard

ENGLISH MARITIME WRITING:
Hakluyt to Cook: Oliver Warner

THE ENGLISH SHORT STORY I: & II:
T. O. Beachcroft

THE ENGLISH SONNET: P. Cruttwell

ENGLISH SERMONS: Arthur Pollard

ENGLISH TRAVELLERS IN THE
NEAR EAST: Robin Fedden

THREE WOMEN DIARISTS: M. Willy

Sixteenth Century and Earlier:

FRANCIS BACON: J. Max Patrick

BEAUMONT & FLETCHER: Ian Fletcher

CHAUCER: Nevill Coghill

RICHARD HOOKER: A. Pollard

THOMAS KYD: Philip Edwards

LANGLAND: Nevill Coghill

LYLY & PEELE: G. K. Hunter

MALORY: M. C. Bradbrook

MARLOWE: Philip Henderson

SIR THOMAS MORE: E. E. Reynolds

RALEGH: Agnes Latham

SIDNEY: Kenneth Muir

SKELTON: Peter Green

SPENSER: Rosemary Freeman

THREE 14TH-CENTURY ENGLISH
MYSTICS: Phyllis Hodgson

TWO SCOTS CHAUCERIANS:
H. Harvey Wood

WYATT: Sergio Baldi

Seventeenth Century:

SIR THOMAS BROWNE: Peter Green

BUNYAN: Henri Talon

CAVALIER POETS: Robin Skelton

CONGREVE: Bonamy Dobrée

DONNE: F. Kermode

DRYDEN: Bonamy Dobrée

ENGLISH DIARISTS:
Evelyn and Pepys: M. Willy

FARQUHAR: A. J. Farmer

JOHN FORD: Clifford Leech

GEORGE HERBERT: T. S. Eliot

HERRICK: John Press

HOBBES: T. E. Jessop

BEN JONSON: J. B. Bamborough

LOCKE: Maurice Cranston

ANDREW MARVELL: John Press

MILTON: E. M. W. Tillyard

RESTORATION COURT POETS:
V. de S. Pinto

SHAKESPEARE: C. J. Sisson

CHRONICLES: Clifford Leech

EARLY COMEDIES: Derek Traversi

LATER COMEDIES: G. K. Hunter

FINAL PLAYS: F. Kermode

HISTORIES: L. C. Knights

POEMS: F. T. Prince

PROBLEM PLAYS: Peter Ure

ROMAN PLAYS: T. J. B. Spencer

GREAT TRAGEDIES: Kenneth Muir

THREE METAPHYSICAL POETS:
Margaret Willy

IZAAK WALTON: Margaret Bottrall

WEBSTER: Ian Scott-Kilvert

WYCHERLEY: P. F. Vernon

Eighteenth Century:

BERKELEY: T. E. Jessop

BLAKE: Kathleen Raine

BOSWELL: P. A. W. Collins

BURKE: T. E. Utley

BURNS: David Daiches

WM. COLLINS: Oswald Doughty

COWPER: N. Nicholson

CRABBE: R. L. Brett

DEFOE: J. R. Sutherland

FIELDING: John Butt

GAY: Oliver Warner

GIBBON: C. V. Wedgwood

GOLDSMITH: A. Norman Jeffares

GRAY: R. W. Ketton-Cremer

HUME: Montgomery Belgion

JOHNSON: S. C. Roberts

POPE: Ian Jack

RICHARDSON: R. F. Brissenden

SHERIDAN: W. A. Darlington

CHRISTOPHER SMART: G. Grigson

SMOLLETT: Laurence Brander

STEELE, ADDISON: A. R. Humphreys

STERNE: D. W. Jefferson

SWIFT: J. Middleton Murry

SIR JOHN VANBRUGH: Bernard Harris

HORACE WALPOLE: Hugh Honour

Nineteenth Century:

MATTHEW ARNOLD: Kenneth Allott

JANE AUSTEN: S. Townsend Warner

BAGEHOT: N. St John-Stevas

THE BRONTË SISTERS: P. Bentley

BROWNING: John Bryson

E. B. BROWNING: Alethea Hayter

SAMUEL BUTLER: G. D. H. Cole

BYRON: Herbert Read

CARLYLE: David Gascoyne

LEWIS CARROLL: Derek Hudson

CLOUGH: Isobel Armstrong
COLERIDGE: Kathleen Raine
CREEVEY & GREVILLE: J. Richardson
DE QUINCEY: Hugh Sykes Davies
DICKENS: K. J. Fielding
  EARLY NOVELS: T. Blount
  LATER NOVELS: B. Hardy
DISRAELI: Paul Bloomfield
GEORGE ELIOT: Lettice Cooper
FERRIER & GALT: W. M. Parker
FITZGERALD: Joanna Richardson
MRS. GASKELL: Miriam Allott
GISSING: A. C. Ward
THOMAS HARDY: R. A. Scott-James
          and C. Day Lewis
HAZLITT: J. B. Priestley
HOOD: Laurence Brander
G. M. HOPKINS: Geoffrey Grigson
T. H. HUXLEY: William Irvine
KEATS: Edmund Blunden
LAMB: Edmund Blunden
LANDOR: G. Rostrevor Hamilton
EDWARD LEAR: Joanna Richardson
MACAULAY: G. R. Potter
MEREDITH: Phyllis Bartlett
JOHN STUART MILL: M. Cranston
WILLIAM MORRIS: P. Henderson
NEWMAN: J. M. Cameron
PATER: Iain Fletcher
PEACOCK: J. I. M. Stewart
ROSSETTI: Oswald Doughty
CHRISTINA ROSSETTI: G. Battiscombe
RUSKIN: Peter Quennell
SIR WALTER SCOTT: Ian Jack
SHELLEY: Stephen Spender
SOUTHEY: Geoffrey Carnall
LESLIE STEPHEN: P. Grosskurth
R. L. STEVENSON: G. B. Stern
SWINBURNE: H. J. C. Grierson
TENNYSON: F. L. Lucas
THACKERAY: Laurence Brander
FRANCIS THOMPSON: P. Butter
TROLLOPE: Hugh Sykes Davies
OSCAR WILDE: James Laver
WORDSWORTH: Helen Darbishire

Twentieth Century:
W. H. AUDEN: Richard Hoggart
HILAIRE BELLOC: Renée Haynes
ARNOLD BENNETT: F. Swinnerton
EDMUND BLUNDEN: Alec M. Hardie
ELIZABETH BOWEN: Jocelyn Brooke
ROBERT BRIDGES: J. Sparrow
ROY CAMPBELL: David Wright
JOYCE CARY: Walter Allen
G. K. CHESTERTON: C. Hollis
WINSTON CHURCHILL: John Connell
R. G. COLLINGWOOD: E. W. F. Tomlin
I. COMPTON-BURNETT: P. H. Johnson

JOSEPH CONRAD: Oliver Warner
WALTER DE LA MARE: K. Hopkins
NORMAN DOUGLAS: Ian Greenlees
T. S. ELIOT: M. C. Bradbrook
FIRBANK & BETJEMAN: J. Brooke
FORD MADOX FORD: Kenneth Young
E. M. FORSTER: Rex Warner
CHRISTOPHER FRY: Derek Stanford
JOHN GALSWORTHY: R. H. Mottram
ROBERT GRAVES: M. Seymour-Smith
GRAHAM GREENE: Francis Wyndham
L. P. HARTLEY & ANTHONY POWELL:
          P. Bloomfield and B. Bergonzi
A. E. HOUSMAN: Ian Scott-Kilvert
ALDOUS HUXLEY: Jocelyn Brooke
HENRY JAMES: Michael Swan
PAMELA HANSFORD JOHNSON:
          Isabel Quigly
JAMES JOYCE: J. I. M. Stewart
RUDYARD KIPLING: Bonamy Dobrée
D. H. LAWRENCE: Kenneth Young
C. DAY LEWIS: Clifford Dyment
WYNDHAM LEWIS: E. W. F. Tomlin
COMPTON MACKENZIE: K. Young
LOUIS MACNEICE: John Press
KATHERINE MANSFIELD: Ian Gordon
JOHN MASEFIELD: L. A. G. Strong
SOMERSET MAUGHAM: J. Brophy
GEORGE MOORE: A. Norman Jeffares
EDWIN MUIR: J. C. Hall
J. MIDDLETON MURRY: Philip Mairet
SEAN O'CASEY: W. A. Armstrong
GEORGE ORWELL: Tom Hopkinson
POETS OF 1939-45 WAR: R. N. Currey
POWYS BROTHERS: R. C. Churchill
J. B. PRIESTLEY: Ivor Brown
HERBERT READ: Francis Berry
FOUR REALIST NOVELISTS: V. Brome
BERNARD SHAW: A. C. Ward
EDITH SITWELL: John Lehmann
OSBERT SITWELL: Roger Fulford
KENNETH SLESSOR: C. Semmler
C. P. SNOW: William Cooper
STRACHEY: R. A. Scott-James
SYNGE & LADY GREGORY:
          Elizabeth Coxhead
DYLAN THOMAS: G. S. Fraser
EDWARD THOMAS: Vernon Scannell
G. M. TREVELYAN: J. H. Plumb
WAR POETS: 1914-18: E. Blunden
EVELYN WAUGH: Christopher Hollis
H. G. WELLS: Montgomery Belgion
PATRICK WHITE: R. F. Brissenden
CHARLES WILLIAMS: J. Heath-Stubbs
ANGUS WILSON: K. W. Gransden
VIRGINIA WOOLF: B. Blackstone
W. B. YEATS: G. S. Fraser
ANDREW YOUNG & R. S. THOMAS:
          L. Clark and R. G. Thomas